Get fit, D

Dan runs to the hut.

Dan runs to the log.

Dan hops on the log.

Go up to the top.

Dan runs to the top.

Dan is fit
but Dan is hot.

Dan sips and sips.

Get fit, Dan!

Level 2: Story 15

Before reading

Say the sounds: g o b h e r f u l
Ensure children use the pure sounds for the consonants without the added "uh" sound, e.g. "llll" not "luh".

Practise blending the sounds: top fit hot runs log hut set sips hops hop run Dan

High-frequency words: get but up it and on did **Tricky words:** the is go to

Vocabulary check: fit – What does it mean to "be fit" or "to get fit"? What does "Get set, go!" mean? When is this used? top – What different meanings does this word have? Discuss the meaning of "top" in different contexts, e.g. I am wearing a red top. She took the top off the bottle.

Story discussion: Look at the cover. Who is this story about? What does the title tell us about this story? What kind of things could Dan do to get fit?

Teaching points: Discuss the use of speech and thought bubbles in this story to show the talking (speech) or thoughts of a character. Ask children to find examples in the book. Introduce the purpose of an exclamation mark to show emphasis. Review "s" on the end of a verb, e.g. hop/hops.

After reading

Comprehension:
- What are some of the things Dan did to get fit?
- How was Sam helping Dan?
- What was Sam holding in his hand? What does a stopwatch do?
- Can you think of other things you can do to help keep yourself fit?

Fluency: Speed read the words again from the inside front cover.